Write It Right

Writing and Giving a Speech

By Cecilia Minden and Kate Roth

Published in the United States of America by
Cherry Lake Publishing
Ann Arbor, Michigan
www.cherrylakepublishing.com

Reading Adviser: Marla Conn MS, Ed., Literacy specialist, Read-Ability, Inc.
Book Designer: Felicia Macheske
Character Illustrator: Carol Herring

Photo Credits: © wavebreakmedia/Shutterstock.com, 5; © areetham/Shutterstock.com, 9; © Pressmaster/Shutterstock.com, 11; © Phovoir/Shutterstock.com, 13; © By Monkey Business Images/Shutterstock.com, 21

Graphics Throughout: © simple surface/Shutterstock.com; © Mix3r/Shutterstock.com; © Artefficient/Shutterstock.com; © lemony/Shutterstock.com; © Svetolk/Shutterstock.com; © EV-DA/Shutterstock.com; © briddy/Shutterstock.com; © IreneArt/Shutterstock.com

Copyright © 2019 by Cherry Lake Publishing
All rights reserved. No part of this book may be reproduced or utilized in any form or by any means without written permission from the publisher.

Library of Congress Cataloging-in-Publication Data

Names: Minden, Cecilia, author. | Roth, Kate, author. | Herring, Carol, illustrator.
Title: Writing and giving a speech / by Cecilia Minden and Kate Roth ; Illustrated by Carol Herring.
Description: Ann Arbor, Michigan : Cherry Lake Publishing, [2019] | Series: Write it right | Includes bibliographical references and index. | Audience: K to grade 3.
Identifiers: LCCN 2018037383| ISBN 9781534142879 (hardcover) | ISBN 9781534139435 (pbk.) | ISBN 9781534140639 (pdf) | ISBN 9781534141834 (hosted ebook)
Subjects: LCSH: Speechwriting—Juvenile literature. | Public speaking—Juvenile literature.
Classification: LCC PN4142 .M564 2019 | DDC 808.5/1—dc23
LC record available at https://lccn.loc.gov/2018037383

Cherry Lake Publishing would like to acknowledge the work of The Partnership for 21st Century Skills. Please visit *www.p21.org* for more information.

Printed in the United States of America
Corporate Graphics

Table of Contents

CHAPTER ONE
I Have to Give a Speech! ... 4

CHAPTER TWO
Speak About What You Know! ... 6

CHAPTER THREE
Get Their Attention ... 8

CHAPTER FOUR
Building the Body of Your Speech ... 12

CHAPTER FIVE
Wrapping Everything Up ... 16

CHAPTER SIX
Practice, Practice, Practice ... 18

GLOSSARY ... 22
FOR MORE INFORMATION ... 23
INDEX ... 24
ABOUT THE AUTHORS ... 24

CHAPTER ONE

I Have to Give a Speech!

Many people are afraid of giving a **speech**. There is no need to be afraid. With a little planning, you can give a speech with **confidence**!

First, ask yourself a few questions. Why are you giving this speech? Is it for a class project? Is it for a club or sports team? Knowing the **purpose** of the speech helps you plan what you want to say.

A speech is a way for one person to speak to many others.

Think about what you want your speech to accomplish.

CHAPTER TWO

Speak About What You Know!

Giving a speech is one way of sharing what you know with others. Speeches are different from reports. People read written reports. They listen to speeches. Think about how you speak to others as you write your speech. Keep your sentences short. Choose your words carefully. Too many details make it hard for the **audience** to keep up with you.

Let's say you are asked to give a 3-to-5-minute speech to your class. How will you choose a **topic**? It is always best to talk about what you know. Why not write about a favorite hobby or activity?

Who will be listening to your speech?

ACTIVITY

Choose a Topic!

HERE'S WHAT YOU'LL NEED:

- A pencil and paper (or a computer and a printer)

INSTRUCTIONS:

1. Make a list of your favorite hobbies or activities.
2. Choose one hobby or activity for your speech.
3. Now list everything that is interesting about the hobby or activity.
4. Read over this second list. What points would interest your classmates the most?

Speech Topic Ideas

- Playing Soccer ✓
- Watching Movies
- Building a Robot

Sample List of Topics

1. The most popular sport in the world ✓
2. Olympic soccer teams
3. Famous soccer fields around the world
4. A famous soccer player

CHAPTER THREE

Get Their Attention

Some speakers begin their speech with an interesting fact or a story. Others begin with a quote or a question. These are all ways you can get the audience's **attention**.

You should also tell the audience what your speech will be about. It is important to include why they should listen to your talk.

ACTIVITY

Write the Opening!

HERE'S WHAT YOU'LL NEED:

- Books or articles about your topic
- A pencil and paper (or a computer and a printer)

INSTRUCTIONS:

1. Read books, articles, or websites that deal with your topic. Use what you learn to create a list of different ways to open your speech.
2. Find a quote about your topic and write it down.
3. Pick an interesting fact about your topic and write it down.
4. Come up with a question about your topic and write it down.
5. Look over your list and choose the best way to open your speech. Start writing!

Opening your speech can also be called "breaking the ice."

Sample List of Openings

QUOTE:

"No individual can win a game by himself." —Pele

INTERESTING FACT:

Soccer played in the United States as we know it today originated in England.

QUESTION:

What is the most popular sport around the world?

Sample Opening Statement

What is the most popular sport in the world? Many think it is football or baseball. It is not! The most popular sport around the world is soccer!

Imagine you are in the audience—
what would grab your attention?

CHAPTER FOUR

Building the Body of Your Speech

You have an opening that will get the audience's attention! Now you must write the **body** of your speech. Choose three main points about your topic that you plan to discuss.

First, name the points. Then tell more about each of them. This helps the audience follow your speech. Think about the order of your main points. As you write, try to link the main points together.

You may want to use **visual aids**. Make sure that everyone in the audience will be able to see the visual aids. Do not pass around objects during your speech. The audience might pay more attention to the objects than to the speaker!

A map helps your audience visualize locations.

ACTIVITY

Write the Body!

HERE'S WHAT YOU'LL NEED:

- A pencil and paper (or a computer and a printer)

INSTRUCTIONS:

1. Write the three main points you want to put in your speech.
2. Explain the first point.
3. Explain the second point.
4. Explain the third point.
4. Read aloud what you've written. Does it make sense? Will your audience understand?

Sample Points to Put in Body

Where did soccer originate?

What are the basic rules of soccer?

Why is soccer so popular around the world?

Sample Explanation of a Main Point

Soccer was created long ago in China from a game called *tsu chu*. *Tsu* means "to kick with your feet." *Chu* means "a ball made of leather." The goal was to kick the ball through a hole in a net. Players could not touch the ball with their hands.

CHAPTER FIVE

Wrapping Everything Up

A strong ending to your speech helps the audience remember what you have said. You should repeat your main points. Some speakers even repeat their opening lines to bring the speech "full circle." That means something has returned to the way it began. Finally, always thank the audience for listening to you.

Looking at your audience and speaking clearly helps to hold their attention.

ACTIVITY

Write the Ending!

HERE'S WHAT YOU'LL NEED:

- A pencil and paper (or a computer and a printer)

INSTRUCTIONS:

1. Restate the main points of your speech.
2. Write a strong final sentence. One idea is to repeat your opening lines.
3. Thank your audience.

Sample Ending

Now you know a few things about soccer. You know it was first played in China. You know a little about how the game is played today. You know that soccer is played more than any other sport. Next time *you* are playing soccer, think about others who are playing the same game all over the world. Thank you.

CHAPTER SIX

Practice, Practice, Practice

You finished writing your speech! Now you need to **rehearse** it out loud. Some speakers use small note cards to help them remember key points. Just try to speak naturally.

You should also practice with your visual aids. Remember to look at the audience and not the visual aids. You may want to invite friends and family members to listen to you practice. They can tell you what they think and offer suggestions. Ask them to time you if you have been given a time limit. Make sure your speech does not run over the limit!

Practicing will make you more confident. You will soon discover that speaking in front of an audience is fun. Giving speeches helps you learn skills that you will use for the rest of your life!

ACTIVITY

Rehearse!

HERE'S WHAT YOU'LL NEED:

- A copy of your speech
- Note cards
- A pencil

INSTRUCTIONS:

1. Write the opening of your speech on a note card.
2. Write each of the three main points on separate note cards.
3. Write the ending on a note card.
4. Write what visual aids you want to use and when.
5. Rehearse your speech several times using the note cards and visual aids.
6. Ask friends and family members to listen to you and time you!

Sample Note Card

MAIN POINT #2:

How is soccer played?

Remember to show the audience the soccer ball, shin guards, and soccer shoes.

ACTIVITY

Make Sure You Didn't Miss Anything!

Ask yourself these questions as you rehearse your speech:

- Do I have an attention-getting opening?
- Do I tell the audience what my speech is about in the opening?
- Do I limit myself to discussing three main points?
- Do I repeat the main points in the end?
- Do I have a strong ending that helps the audience remember what I said?
- Do I remember to thank the audience?
- Do I stay within my time limit?
- Do I know when and where to include my visual aids?

Practice makes perfect!

GLOSSARY

attention (uh-TEN-shuhn) the act of looking at and listening to a speaker

audience (AW-dee-uhns) a group of listeners

body (BAH-dee) the main part of a speech

confidence (KAHN-fih-duhns) believing in yourself and your ability to achieve something

purpose (PUR-puhs) goal

rehearse (rih-HURS) practice

speech (SPEECH) a planned presentation before an audience

topic (TAH-pik) subject

visual aids (VIZH-oo-uhl AYDZ) materials that the audience can look at during a speech

For More INFORMATION

BOOKS

Bullard, Lisa. *Ace Your Oral or Multimedia Presentation*. Berkeley Heights, NJ: Enslow Publishers, 2009.

WEBSITES

Best Speech Topics—Speech Topics for Kids
www.best-speech-topics.com/speech-topics-for-kids.html
Check out this site for countless cool speech subjects.

Famous Speeches and Speech Topics
www.famous-speeches-and-speech-topics.info
Read famous speeches as well as tips on public speaking.

INDEX

audience, 6, 20
   getting their attention, 8, 11
   thanking, 16

body of speech, 12–15
   sample points, 15
   "breaking the ice," 9

confidence, 4, 18

ending, speech, 16–17

main points, 12, 15, 16–17

note cards, 18, 19

opening, speech, 8–11
   repeating, 16
   sample, 10

practice, 18–21
   questions to ask during, 20

speech
   benefits of, 18
   body of, 12–15
   ending, 16–17
   how it's different from report, 6
   opening, 8–11, 16

speech (*cont.*)
   practicing, 18–21
   purpose of, 4–5
   topic, 6–7
   visual aids, 12–13, 18

time limits, 18

topic, 6–7
   choosing main points about, 12
   sample points, 15

visual aids, 12–13, 18

About the AUTHORS

Cecilia Minden is the former director of the Language and Literacy Program at Harvard Graduate School of Education. She earned her doctorate from the University of Virginia. While at Harvard, Dr. Minden also taught several writing courses. Her research focused on early literacy skills and developing phonics curriculums. She is now a literacy consultant and the author of over 100 books for children. Dr. Minden lives with her family in McKinney, Texas. She enjoys helping students become interested in reading and writing.

Kate Roth has a doctorate from Harvard University in language and literacy and a master's degree from Columbia University Teachers College in curriculum and teaching. Her work focuses on writing instruction in the primary grades. She has taught kindergarten, first grade, and Reading Recovery. She has also instructed hundreds of teachers from around the world in early literacy practices. She lived with her husband and three children in China for many years, and now they live in Connecticut.